It's All About Service!

Successfully Dealing with Difficult People

If we can master that which is most difficult, everything else will become second nature.

It's All About Service!
Successfully Dealing with Difficult People

Cover image courtesy of Pixabay. Used with permission.

Send inquires about this or other material to: canfieldwritingservice@gmail.com.

ISBN-13: 978-1500189907
ISBN-10: 1500189901

COMPANY NAME_____

YOUR NAME_____

DATE OF TRAINING_____

SUPERVISOR/INSTRUCTOR_____

CONTENTS

1   Customer Service   1

2   The Complainer   5

3   I Want Everything Free!   11

4   The Legitimate Complaint   17

5   The Ten Commandments of Human Relations   21

6   Simple Keys to Relieve Stress   31

When I was young, I used to admire intelligent people; as I grow older, I admire kind people. - *Abraham Joshua Heschel*

There is overwhelming evidence that the higher the level of self-esteem, the more likely one will be to treat others with respect, kindness, and generosity. - *Nathaniel Branden*

The worst sin toward our fellow creatures is not to hate them, but to be indifferent to them—that's the essence of inhumanity: - *George Bernard Shaw*

A kind heart is a fountain of gladness, making everything in its vicinity freshen into smiles. - *Washington Irving*

CUSTOMER
SERVICE

$\mathcal{S}$*uccess*

Customer - One who enters a shop to buy.

Service - State of being a servant; work done for, and benefit conferred on another; act of kindness.

Question: Is the customer *always* right?

Answer: The customer *always being right* is a mathematical impossibility.

What is meant by the old adage *"the customer is always right"*? Any reasonable person knows that the customer cannot always be right. What is usually meant when we say the *customer is always right* is that we will do whatever we can to satisfy the customer's need (within the boundaries of a company's policies, proper ethics, and the law). In other words, we make them *feel* as if they're right as we attempt to satisfy them the best we know how.

Accomplishing this task, while being honest and forthright, is one of the many challenges of customer service. The task of satisfying customers in order to increase our customer base becomes even more difficult when dealing with the variety of personalities existing in the world.

In this study we will examine three types of difficult customers. We will also examine the interpersonal skills needed to deal with each one. The three types of difficult customers are:

1. The *never satisfied* customer

2. The *"I want everything free"* customer

3. The legitimate complaint.

We will also study the *Ten Commandments of Human Relations* along with several organizational keys that can assist in alleviating stress in the workplace, and which can ultimately relieve stress in other areas of our lives.

Following the suggestions put forth in this study should not only lead to a better understanding of how to successfully deal with the public and stay organized while managing our time more effectively; but most importantly we can learn how to leave our emotions at work so that we will have less work-related stress invading our private lives.

Success Quote - "I will pay more for the ability to deal with people than for any other ability under the sun." - *John D. Rockefeller*

Participant Roundtable

- What are some of the most difficult challenges you've encountered in dealing with customers?

- How would you evaluate your response to the situation (e.g. was it handled professionally, a mediocre response, or a poor response)?

- What was the final outcome of the most difficult customer situation (i.e. was the customer satisfied, dissatisfied, etc.)?

- If the situation ended negatively, how did it affect your attitude?

Notes

THE COMPLAINER

It may be difficult for some to imagine, but *there are* people in the world who love to complain. As a matter of fact there are some people we would swear are trying to turn complaining into an art form. For example, these are the types of people we may encounter on the most beautiful, sunny, warm day of spring (a day when birds are chirping and the freshness of new life is in the air), and yet they complain while pointing out every negative aspect they can think of.

Bestselling author and speaker John Mason said:

> A life of complaining is the ultimate rut. Ask yourself, "How many successful complainers do I know?" Someone else once said, "Little men with little minds and little imagination go through life in little ruts, smugly resisting all changes which would jar their little worlds."

People act in ways determined by many factors—factors which are *outside of our control*. In our brief encounters with others of the human race, it's important to remember one of life's central truths: *We cannot change people.* Each individual chooses how they will act on a daily basis.

Therefore, there's absolutely no need to take the problems of others on our shoulders as if we're responsible for all the ills of society.

The aforementioned seems very simple, yet how many of us take the problems of others on ourselves? Furthermore, how can we determine if we're carrying the problems of others on our shoulders? One way is to ask ourselves a couple of simple questions:

1. Do we argue with people in our heads *after the fact?*

2. Are we losing sleep following a bad day at work after we've attempted to please people who cannot be pleased; or after encountering those who have no desire to be satisfied?

Additionally, we must recognize that our brief encounters will probably never make lasting changes to a customer's innate personality. Customer service professionals should avoid trying to assume the role of an amateur physiologist. So, where does that leave us? While it's certainly good to have a positive attitude toward others, if we're not careful we can end up allowing their problems or bad attitudes to impact our lives in a negative manner; and then we can end up carrying those things around like expensive baggage for which we have no storage.

> Success Quote: "For peace of mind, resign as general manager of the universe." - *Larry Eisenberg*

There are several simple rules we can observe when dealing with the serial complainer.

1. Don't Take it Personally

We must remember that the professional complainer isn't attacking us, they're attacking the whole world of which we just happen to be a part of. The truth is most expert complainers don't really want to be satisfied. What they really want is to be heard. Generally speaking, once this type of person has made their statement or complaint they will retreat. Once again, we shouldn't take it personally. They're not mad at us, per se. For whatever reason they're mad at the world. Allow the trained professionals to figure out all the motivations, reasons, and cures for personality disorders. One who is working in customer service is simply rising to the challenge of walking these individuals through their momentary crisis to a reasonable resolution.

It is possible that the professional complainer can become heightened emotionally. If this type of person doesn't retreat, it might be necessary to call the authorities to have them removed. Of course if the situation deteriorates to that level, employees should follow company policies concerning notification of managers and the proper authorities. It's also wise to alert other employees so that they may witness our actions. Most importantly we must *keep our cool.* We should always occupy the *high ground* (i.e. a calm voice and non-threatening body language).

If we take complaints or harsh words personally it will surely have an impact on our personal lives. Learning to allow complaints to roll off our backs takes discipline on the part of the customer service representative. Yet, if we don't develop that ability, it can affect our longevity within the industry.

> Survival tip: *It's not your problem, so don't take it home with you!*

Undoubtedly, to some people this survival tip may sound cold and hard. But we must remember we're talking about our emotional well-being. As already stated, whether or not we leave our problems at work will have an influence on our long-term survival in the business world.

2. Don't ever stoop to their level.

The first mistake in dealing with the complainer is taking what they're saying personally. If we can avoid making the first mistake, then hopefully we can avoid the making the second.

The complainer wants us to stoop to his level. Misery not only loves company—it wants ours. Complainers attract other complainers. Pulling someone else into their gloomy world actually makes a complainer feel better. If we stoop to that level, it not only feeds the complainers ego (because they know their words have affected us), but it also reassures them that they're not alone in their world of misery.

Staying positive not only helps the customer service representative maintain a tone of professionalism, but it also conveys to the complainer that not everyone will give in to their tactics. If, in fact, the complainer is able to pull us down to his level, soon we will find ourselves engaged in a two-person pity party. The danger in wallowing in their complaints is that our own attitude toward our company can quickly change. Too often when an employee finds themselves continually agreeing with the complainers about the company's policies and practices, they themselves become discontent in the workplace. This not only serves to undermine our own morale, but it also gives the complainer fuel for their fire.

A customer service representative must not only know the company's policies, but also stand by them while not giving in to the consummate complainer.

> Success Quote: "Wisdom is the quality that keeps you from getting into situations where you need it." - *Doug Larson*

3. Never give in to unsubstantiated complaints.

If a disgruntled customer has no legitimate basis for their complaint, and we've exhausted all of our company's policies and procedures to appease them but their issue cannot be resolved; then we must simply end the exchange as pleasantly as possible. To conclude the matter, we might consider using phrases like:

"I appreciate what you're saying, however there's simply nothing I can do for you."

-or-

"I wish I could help you, but our company policy simply will not allow it."

When we place the final decision on the broad shoulders of the company, we might possibly save our relationship with the customer. In turn, this might cause even the most difficult customer to return to the business with a different attitude simply because *we were understanding and polite*. Companies (especially large ones) can appear to be somewhat impersonal to the average consumer. Therefore, the customer service representative becomes the face of the company to the consumer—meaning what they see and the voice they hear. The customer's memory of the service rendered will primarily be based upon their dealings with the individual representative of the company, taking into account the empathy and attitude with which the customer service representative resolved their situation.

> Success Quote: "Tact is the ability to step on someone's shoes without messing up their shine." - *John Maxwell*

Participant Roundtable

- Discuss some other words or phrases that will help diffuse an encounter with a complaining customer.

- What policies does your company have in place to "satisfy" (or deal with) the complaining customer if their complaint has no grounds?

- What happens if a company gives in to unsubstantiated complaints by refunding money or providing services without remuneration?

- How do you plan to insulate yourself from becoming angry or pessimistic after dealing with complainers?

Notes

I WANT EVERYTHING FREE!

Just like there are those in this world who love to complain, there are also people who think they should get everything free. Our fast-paced and cyber-active society has a subculture who not only want everything for free, but who have also learned how to manipulate people or systems into providing it for them.

We don't have to work in customer service long before we develop the skill of spotting those that desire a free ride. Keep in mind that an individual who desires a free ride is not limited to one particular socio-economic class. Those who work in customer service encounter people from all walks of life who will attempt to get all they can possibly have for free. How should we respond when we're dealing with this type of individual?

Consider the following when responding to this type of individual.

1. Keep your cool.

The person who feels they should receive something for nothing can upset us just as quickly as the professional complainer. As a customer service professional, we must always occupy the high ground. An unwavering characteristic which should be threaded throughout every situation involving our customers is: *Always be a professional.* A professional is a person who has invested the time and effort to develop the skills necessary for the task, and those developed skills have become habits.

Staying calm in difficult situations is one of the many hallmarks of professionalism. Furthermore, exhibiting grace under pressure can be very intimidating to any difficult customer. If we don't allow them to "rattle" us (i.e. make us angry or unsure of our decisions), then we're communicating that we are in control of our emotions. When the complainer or the free-loader observes that we're in control of our emotions, we send them a clear message that we cannot be manipulated into giving in to their manipulation or fraud.

> Success Quote: "Nothing gives one person so much advantage over another as to remain always cool and unruffled under all circumstances." - *Thomas Jefferson*

2. Know our limits and stick to them.

How much time do we spend with the person who wants something for nothing? With sufficient evidence, a business can prosecute a shoplifter. But what about the person who isn't shoplifting? What about the person who tries to manipulate a free gift certificate, or a decreased payment on their account simply because they feel they deserve it? This person might end up becoming a legitimate long-term customer if they're handled correctly.

Solid professional conduct is the key. For the customer service representative this means no raised voice, no tit-for-tat, constant empathy and understanding for the customer, and making every attempt to diffuse a bad situation. Once our professional conduct is observed, and they recognize we will not budge concerning our company's policies, then a clear line of understanding has been established. Not only must *we know* our limits, *but so should the customer*. After we've explained our company's policies, then they must be reinforced by means of courtesy and kindness.

> Webster's Dictionary defines *courtesy* as excellence of manners or behavior; politeness.

Courtesy is an outward expression of respect. No matter what type of customer we deal with, courtesy and respect must always be present. That's where customer service becomes extremely challenging. Company policy defines our limitations concerning customer transactions, however it's courtesy and kindness that determine the amount of success we will have in any business dealing.

The fact is no one likes to be treated rudely. Remember that for every one customer we offend, in reality we have just offended ten. Why? Because typically one offended customer will tell *at least ten* of their friends. There are not many businesses that can continually withstand an unfriendly reputation.

That being the case, how can we deal with the person who wants a free ride? When it becomes clear what they're trying to do, the simplest response is to *smile* and politely say, *"Sir/ma'am, I'm really sorry, but that's just not possible."* Then, reiterate why it isn't possible while pointing them toward a product or service that will sufficiently and economically meet their needs. It is important for the customer to know that we desire to meet their needs, even though we cannot do it in the manner they desire.

The bottom line is, if we give in to those who think they should have everything for free (or discounted), we will undoubtedly encounter ten or more of their friends who will expect the same treatment. A refusal with a friendly smile, kindly spoken words, and perhaps a little humor, will stop the free-loader while possibly retaining a customer. Who knows, they may even become a customer who doesn't expect a free ride.

> Success Quote: "The most important single ingredient in the formula of success is knowing how to get along with people." - *Theodore Roosevelt*

Participant Roundtable

- How often do you encounter customers who feel they deserve something for nothing?

- Are there other ways of dealing with those who always want something for nothing?

- Do you think it's possible to turn these types of situations around so that those who think they deserve a free ride will actually become customers who see the value in our products and services and are willing to pay for them?

- What are your company's policies for dealing with those who think they deserve credit, money back, or free services simply because an error occurred?

- Do you feel that those who work alongside of you are familiar with these company policies? Why or why not?

Notes

THE LEGITIMATE COMPLAINT

Just as there are those who wallow in the world of complaining, and those who constantly want a free ride, there are also those who have legitimate complaints. These are generally well-meaning people who are possibly a little upset because they feel they have been slighted.

A person who has a legitimate complaint is the very situation where we must have the attitude that the customer is always right. This person should be given our full attention. Initially this customer may be somewhat difficult to deal with. However, if handled correctly they will not only walk away satisfied, they might even recommend our business to their friends.

When dealing with legitimate complaints, one of the challenges for those in customer service is not developing any type of attitude when responding to the complaint. If we maintain a professional disposition toward the customer as we investigate whether they have a legitimate complaint, then we can proceed in a way that will be extremely satisfying for the customer.

Once we've uncovered a legitimate complaint, every effort should be made to correct the situation as promptly as possible. Using affirming phrases like, *"You're absolutely correct,"* will not only calm the customer, but it will also give them some of the satisfaction they're looking for. The customer must be assured that we're doing everything possible to solve the problem.

For the customer service professional this can, *and should be* one of the most rewarding customer encounters. In these types of situations we can not only freely and genuinely extend courtesy and kindness, but we can also put to work our problem-solving skills in a way that will shine a favorable light on ourselves and our company.

> Success Quote: "Natural talent, intelligence, a wonderful education—none of these guarantees success. Something else is needed: The sensitivity to understand what other people want and the willingness to give it to them." - *John Luther*

Participant Roundtable

- What are some of the successes you've had with solving problems for customers with legitimate complaints?

- How did you investigate the complaint to uncover whether or not it was legitimate?

- What are some of the phrases or actions you've employed that have led to the successful resolution of legitimate complaints?

- How did the customer respond? Did they walk away thankful and satisfied, or did they leave still having a bad attitude toward the company?

- What policies does your company have in place to satisfy this type of complaint?

Notes

THE TEN COMMANDMENTS OF HUMAN RELATIONS[1]

The Ten Commandments of Human Relations are a somewhat well-known basis for how to treat others with respect. The group leader or instructor should encourage open discussion within the group concerning each of these basic elements. John Wooden, one of the most successful college basketball coaches of his time, said whenever one of his teams was losing, he would always take them back to the fundamentals. Though these ten aspects of how to treat others are basic, it's always good to be reminded of them and how they will lead to success.

> Success Quote: "It's the little details that are vital. Little things make big things happen." – *John Wooden*

1. Speak *to* People

There's nothing worse for a customer than dealing with a business representative who doesn't look them in the eyes. People who refuse to look at us as we speak to them are communicating a high degree of insincerity. There is also an innate suspicion that's generally attached to those who won't look us in the eyes.

No matter what position we occupy in a company, we must attempt to speak *to* people and not at them or around them. Customers need to know we're not only talking but we're also listening. Most customers will appreciate being able to readily observe the sincerity in our eyes. Most customers have a need to feel a sense of genuineness in those with whom they're doing business.

> Success Quote: "Most communication problems can be solved with proximity." - *Benjamin Franklin*

2. Smile at People

A customer's first impression can determine whether or not they will do business with us, and whether they will recommend us to a friend. A warm and friendly smile, in addition to a firm handshake, will speak volumes.

When we apply these valuable tools, we've just welcomed the customer into our world with kindness and respect. We've made them feel at home and let them know (*through non-verbal communication*) that we desire to help them in any way we can.

A smile also conveys that we enjoy our job. If a customer sees that we enjoy working in the business they've just entered, they will feel it's a place that's enjoyable to do business. Our attitude and body language can create a comfortable and inviting atmosphere. If a customer feels at home in our place of business, they're more likely to return and even tell their friends. A warm smile can accomplish so much!

> Success Quote: "Kindness is a language which the deaf can hear and the blind can see." - *Unknown*

3. Call People by Name

There are those among us who are not very skilled at learning and remembering a person's name. Nevertheless, every effort should be made to remember a customer's name *and use it*. We should also be careful not to *overuse* a person's name. Overusing someone's name can sound very disingenuous (e.g. *"Well John...let me tell you John...this is the best gadget John that has ever been invented..."*).

Overusing a person's name in a conversation can be the result of insecurity or simply the manifestation of a nervous habit. This behavior should be avoided. It not only sounds very insincere, but it will also reveal that we're nervous or we're trying too hard. Subsequently, this type of behavior sends a message that we're not as competent as we ought to be. (We know that certain habits must be overcome, and overcoming them takes time and practice. Yet, recognizing we need to work on such things is the first step.)

A warm smile and a firm handshake while looking a customer in the eyes is a great beginning. Then, using the customer's name in a *sincere manner* will more than likely put us on the right track.

> Success Quote: "People aren't sales resistant—they are salespeople resistant." - *Mark Hebenstreit*

4. Be Friendly and Helpful

One would think that being friendly and helpful are the most obvious tools in customer service. Nevertheless, how many times have we entered a store to buy something and then waited for ten minutes until someone offers to help us? How often have we explained what we need, but the person behind the counter never bothers to look at us or even investigate our need? What's even worse if we receive a reply in a sarcastic or bothered tone such as, "I'm sorry, we don't carry that!" To add insult to injury, some customer service representatives have been guilty of accompanying their snide reply with a smirk on their face or a rolling of their eyes.

Forty to fifty years ago, being friendly and helpful would've been obvious and expected traits for any human relations—especially in the area of customer service. However, in today's world it seems to be a lost art. If we desire to be successful in any area of customer service *we must be friendly and helpful.*

We must always remember that customers *are not interrupting our day*. They're simply calling upon us to perform the service for which we are employed and they are desiring to pay for. Performing that service while be friendly and helpful exhibits true professionalism as well as extending to the customer the courtesy and respect they deserve.

> Success Quote: "Be a yardstick of quality. Some people aren't used to an environment where excellence is expected." - *Stephen Jobs*

5. Be Cordial

Webster's Dictionary provides us with this definition of the word cordial: *"Expressing warmth of heart; sincere."*

Nobody likes a phony. The best customer service representatives are those who can express sincerity in any situation they encounter. Whether we're saying, *"No, we can't exchange that"*; *"No, we don't have any vacant rooms"*; or we're just telling an amusing story about our dog—we must convey warmth and sincerity. Warmth, sincerity, and an understanding heart are the characteristics of a great customer service representative. These are the ones who will undoubtedly be thought of very highly by their customers, and valued by the company they work for.

> Success Quote: "Few things will pay you bigger dividends than the time and trouble you take to understand people. Almost nothing will add more to your stature as an executive and a person. Nothing will give you greater satisfaction or bring you more happiness." - *Kienzle & Dare*

6. Have a Genuine Interest in People

Once again, this seems like an obvious quality for those engaged in customer service. Nonetheless, how many times have we encountered customer service representatives who give the impression that they have a serious dislike for other human beings? J. A. Holmes said, "It is well to remember that the entire population of the universe *with one trifling exception* is composed of others."

Every now and then we need to be reminded that our customers are also our bread and butter. If we doubt that statement, then imagine doing without them for a short while. Furthermore, if we're doing our best to exhibit the first five of these commandments, then our interest in people will not depend upon how much money they have in their pocketbook. Our interest in people will simply be because...*they are people.*

> Success Quote: "How far you go in life depends on your being tender with the young, compassionate with the aged, sympathetic with the striving, and tolerant of the weak and the strong. Because someday in life you will have been all of these." - *George Washington Carver*

7. Be Generous with Praise

This commandment seems to fly in the face of many of our 21st Century philosophies such as: *"It's a dog eat dog world"*; *"Only the strong survive"*; *"Every man for himself"*; and of course, *"Nice guys finish last."*

Personally, I believe nice guys always finish on top—it just takes them longer because they have no desire to use people or take shortcuts.

Some might argue that we'll never get anywhere in life if we're always praising others. The truth is *one of the best ways to promote yourself is through promoting others*. The most powerful people in Hollywood are not the actors (who undoubtedly are the most well-known), but rather the film directors and producers. Without the power and influence of the directors and producers (who very few are familiar with) the actors would not become famous. *If we make our customers feel like stars, we can be assured that we will be very successful*. That may sound cliché, but it's true. It always works.

How do we accomplish this? It's very simple. Most people's favorite subject is themselves. People love to talk about their new home, their new car, their grandkids, etc. This truth opens up two wonderful avenues for those in customer service.

1. It allows us to learn something about the customer, *which increases the quality of service*.

2. It opens the door for us to praise and promote our customers.

If we're going to be successful, we must learn that this life is not all about satisfying ourselves, but rather it is about meeting the needs of others. One of the greatest ways to develop long-term customers is to learn about their interests and then commend them for the loyalty, commitment, and kindness they've shown to us.

> Success Quote: "A gossip is one who talks to you about others; a bore is one who talks to you about himself; and a brilliant conversationalist is one who talks to you about yourself." - *Lisa Kirk*

8. Be Considerate of the Feelings of Others

Considering the feelings of others is yet another lost art. In today's culture the feelings of others can easily get buried in the fast-paced world of business. Some would argue that all that mushy and touchy-feely stuff belongs on TV, but not in the hardcore business world.

It's true that in most businesses the touchy-feely stuff probably doesn't fit very well. On the other hand, considering the feelings of others can simply mean showing up for a meeting on time so that we don't keep others waiting. It can also mean exercising simple courtesy by calling if we're going to be late for a business luncheon. Other ways might be remembering Secretary's Day; or by acknowledging a customer's birthday or anniversary. Returning phone calls, texts, or emails *promptly* is an excellent way to show consideration to others.

Our reputation will always go before us and our business. Our success will rest upon the courtesy and consideration for which we are known. As we've learned over and over, nobody likes dealing with people who are rude and unmannerly. Courtesy and thoughtfulness should be our calling card.

> Success Quote: "It is one of the most beautiful compensations of this life that no man can sincerely try to help another without helping himself." - *Ralph Waldo Emerson*

9. Be Thoughtful of the Opinions of Others

All of the commandments of human relations obviously apply to anyone who deals with people (i.e. CSR's, CEO's, ministers, police officers, etc.). One thing a professional must always be on the lookout for is arrogance. While we should all desire to be the best at what we do, the fact is most people resist doing business with an arrogant and prideful person (i.e. someone who is bloated with self-importance).

Talking down to people as if they are inferior sends the message that we think we know everything and they have nothing to offer. This is particularly dangerous in customer service. We must listen to the opinions of our customers. In doing this, we not only exhibit respect, but we will also discover their needs.

Typically, a customer service representative who is an arrogant know-it-all will not be successful. The bottom line is, *people are our business, therefore we must be interested their opinions*.

> Success Quote: "You can't make the other fellow feel important in your presence if you secretly feel that he is a nobody." - *Les Giblin*

10. Be Alert to Give Service

Be on the lookout for opportunities! A failure is someone who lumbers through life assuming that opportunities will come to him. On the other hand, a successful person is constantly on the lookout for opportunities. Furthermore, when nothing seems to be happening, he creates opportunities through staying busy and engaged. The simple truth is that success comes through hard work. Thomas Edison said, "Opportunity is missed by most people because it is dressed in overalls and looks like work." There's another old saying that goes: "The way to the throne room is through the servants' quarters." Successful people simply devote time and effort to accomplish what others refuse to do.

Eric Rimshaw said, "We should allow the portrait of our character to be painted on the canvas of excellence." Serving others is not only the beginning, but also the foundation of true success.

> Success Quote: "Commit yourself to excellence from the start. No legacy is so rich as excellence. The quality of your life will be in direct proportion to your commitment to excellence, regardless of what you choose to do." - *John Mason*

Participant Roundtable

- Which of the Ten Commandments of Human Relations do you consider the most important?

- Which one strikes a nerve in your own life? (Which one do you think you need to work on the most?)

- Are these principles practiced regularly in your business?

- In light of these principles, name some ways the company can improve its overall performance.

Notes

SIMPLE KEYS TO RELIEVE STRESS[2]

We know there are many things which can cause stress in our lives. For example:

1. Too much to do and too little time to do it.

2. Problems with other people

3. Family issues

4. Work related issues

5. Financial pressure.

We each handle stress differently. Many times stress relievers in our lives can be unhealthy. For instance, some people overeat; some people stop eating; some people binge on alcohol; some people binge with money; some people lash out in anger; and some people get depressed.

Here are a few simple observations about stress:

1. *Everybody* has stress in their lives.

2. Stress can be a positive or negative experience in our lives. An example of a positive outcome can be seen in certain individuals who clearly work better under pressure.

3. Much negative stress is *unnecessary*.

4. When stress becomes a strain it can become harmful.

It has been said that 40% of what we worry about will never happen. 30% of what we worry about concerns old decisions that can't be changed. 12% is often criticism from people who feel inferior to you (for whatever reason). 10% of our worrying is over health problems which are only made worse by our worrying; and only about 8% of our worries are legitimate problems that we can meet head on.

In his book entitled *Self Talk*, author David Stoop made the following observation:

> 40 million Americans suffer from allergies; 30 million suffer from sleeplessness; 25 million suffer from hyper-tension; 20 million Americans suffer from ulcers. All of it can be traced back to negative stress.

Stoop also suggests that there are many people in medical research that believe 75-90% of all illnesses are cause by the negative stresses of modern day life—these are our responses to those tensions.

Whether one agrees with Stoop's conclusions, the fact remains that stress can be harmful to us in many ways, and it can affect nearly every aspect of our lives.

BASIC PRINCIPLES OF STRESS MANAGEMENT

1. Be Honest with Yourself and Others

A lot of stress in our lives comes from wearing masks and being untruthful with others. Insecurity always produces pressure in our lives because we feel the pressure to perform. If we're not honest with ourselves, then we will allow others to manipulate and pressure us into being something we're not. Trying to live up to the expectations of others will always cause unnecessary stress in our lives. We can relieve a great deal of stress simply by *being ourselves.*

> Consider this quote: "When people are free to do as they please, they usually imitate each other." - *Eric Hoffer*

2. Know *Who* You're Trying to Please

Purpose, vision, and action lead to success. We must stay focused. When we try to please everybody we end up saying yes to too many things. This only leads to frustration and ultimately mediocrity. In trying to please everyone we end up pleasing no one. Then we become frustrated because we're incapable of doing everything for everybody. Next, mediocrity sets in because we cannot concentrate or make firm decisions due to the fact that our abilities are spread so thin.

When we try to please everyone it becomes impossible to be decisive. As a result, our indecision cultivates frustration, which in turn produces confusion. Gordon Graham said, "Decision is a sharp knife that cuts clean and straight; indecision is a dull one that hacks and tears and leaves ragged edges behind." *We must be determined to be decisive.*

3. Don't Run from Risk

This doesn't mean we act foolishly. Foolish risks are those which endanger our lives or the lives of others. Those are not the kinds of risks we should even consider.

On the other hand, how many times have we all avoided even a small risk in our lives in order to avoid stress? When we avoid taking even the smallest risks we wind up even more stressed because then we begin to feel as if life isn't even worth living. In our desire to stay in a "safe place," we end up boxing our dreams in with us. We need to face the fact that life itself is a risk. Life refuses to be neat and clean. We need to be challenged. Challenges produce growth and propel us beyond being average. William M. Winans said, "Not doing more than the average is what keeps the average down."

> Success Quote: "Undertake something that is difficult; it will do you good. Unless you try to do something beyond what you have already mastered, you will never grow." - *Ronald E. Osborn*

4. Set Definite Goals

Anatole France said, "The average man does not know what to do with this life, yet wants another one which will last forever." Unless YOU plan your life and set priorities, you will be pressured by what others think is important. Every day we either live by priorities or we live by pressure. More often than not, being prepared will *prevent* pressure, or it will cause pressure *to work in our favor*.

When we design specific goals, we will not only understand what we're trying to accomplish, but we'll also begin to be more organized. John Mason said, "A goal is a dream with a deadline."

We shouldn't be afraid to dream big dreams! However, we have to remember that no dream was ever fulfilled without definite goals, and specific and deliberate actions.

> Success Quote: "We are told never to cross a bridge till we come to it, but this world is owned by men who have 'crossed bridges' in their imagination far ahead of the crowd." - *Speakers Library*

5. Stay Focused

We all get bogged down from time to time. When we have a number of tasks facing us, many times it works well to focus on one thing at a time. Once we accomplished the first thing, then we move on to the next.

Most successful people are list makers. They create *short-term* lists and *long-term* lists, both of which are very beneficial. If we set goals and make lists, then we can enjoy the great satisfaction of crossing things off our lists while knowing we accomplished something that day. Focus is the vehicle that drives us on the road to accomplishment. We must always stay focused on our goals and never stop until they're completed.

> Success Quote: "Every human mind is a great slumbering power until awakened by a keen specific desire, and by a definite resolution to do." - *Edgar F. Roberts*

6. Capitalize on Your Strengths and Delegate the Rest

Knowing our strengths is important. Understanding and admitting our weaknesses is also important. There are reasons some people insist on doing everything themselves. Normally it can identified in one of two things:

1. Perfectionism

2. Insecurity

Theodore Roosevelt said, "The best executive is the one who has sense enough to pick good men to do what he wants done, and self-restraint enough to keep from meddling with them while they do it."

Of course we should desire to do everything with excellence. However, perfectionism will not only wear us out, but it can also drive those around us a little crazy. If we're going to grow, and allow those around us to grow in their gifts and abilities, then we must delegate tasks that will allow others to learn and even make mistakes. Reportedly, IBM executive Tom Watson was once asked if he was going to fire an employee who made a mistake that cost IBM $600,000. He said, "No. I just spent $600,000 training him. Why would I want somebody to hire his experience?"

It is also important to recognize that there's no such thing as a 'self-made' man. We all need help once in a while. It shows great humility and strength of character to allow others to help us in areas where we're weak. It will also alleviate a great amount of stress in our lives.

> Success Quote: "Here lies a man who knew how to enlist the service of better men than himself." – Inscribed on *Andrew Carnegie's Tombstone*

7. Talk to Someone

There are some people in this world who talk *too much*; and then there are others who *need to talk* with someone. Consider how often we hear news reports containing witness statements which sound something like this: "I didn't know him well. *He was a quiet person who kept to himself*. Though I never would've imagined he'd kill his wife."

Our lives can quickly become like a pressure cooker, especially in this day and age. Human beings weren't meant to be alone. As the old saying goes, "Even the Lone Ranger had Tonto." A true friend is one who not only enjoys your company when you're up, but desires to be there for you when you're down.

In his book, *You're Born An Original, Don't Die a Copy*, John Mason wrote:

> The man who believes in nothing but himself lives in a very small world - one in which few will want to enter. The man who sings his own praises may have the right tune but the wrong lyrics. The higher you go in life, the more dependent you become on other people. Work together with others. Remember the banana: Every time it leaves the bunch, it gets peeled and eaten.

> Success Quote: "Friendship makes prosperity more brilliant, and lightens adversity by dividing and sharing it." - *Cicero*

8. Take Time to Enjoy Life

Time with our families (away from phones, texts, e-mail, and Internet) is *invaluable*. It's true that hard work breeds success, but proper rest and relaxation brings peace of mind which will prolong our lives.

We all need to stop and smell the roses. Life is too short to be consumed with wealth and promotion at the expense of our physical well-being and our relationships with family and friends.

As each moment of our day passes by, as each year ends and a new one begins, we become increasingly more aware of our mortality. We cannot retrieve lost moments. We must make the most of our lives!

> Success Quote: "LOST—Somewhere between sunrise and sunset - one golden hour encrusted with sixty silver minutes, each studded with sixty diamond seconds. No reward is offered. They are lost and gone forever." - *Anonymous*

Participant Roundtable

- Do you find the keys to relieving stress truthful and practical?

- Do you believe it's true that stress is often times manufactured by not taking care of things when we should, or by not managing our time well?

- How many of these items are you doing well, and how many could you possibly do better?

- What other keys to relieving stress would you add to this list?

Notes

Notes

ABOUT THE AUTHOR_____

Jeff Canfield's resume includes six years in the Army National Guard, eight years in municipal law enforcement, and seven years working directly with delinquent youth. Jeff has served faithfully in pastoral ministry since 1999. He has a Masters in Applied Theology and a Doctorate in Ministry from Logos University where he serves as part of the adjunct faculty for distance education.

Jeff is the author of many other books including: *A Call to Honor*, *Life Isn't Rocket Science*, the *Somerset Elm* series (historical Christian fiction in three novellas), *Somerset Elm—Joshua's Journey* (all three novellas in one novel), *The End of the Lane* (Christian fiction), *When Church and Government Collide* (nonfiction), *Men's and Women's Discipleship Journals*, several volumes of *Reproducible Bible Studies*, and he's the coauthor of *What Left Behind Left Out—The Truth* (nonfiction).

Contact Jeff at canfieldwritingservice@gmail.com.

Endnotes

[1] The Ten Commandments of Human Relations, Author Unknown.

[2] 8 Stress Relieving Principles adapted from the book *Self Talk*, by David Stoop, published by Revell, Ada, MI, copyright 1996.

www.ingramcontent.com/pod-product-compliance
Lightning Source LLC
Chambersburg PA
CBHW081621170526
45166CB00009B/3060